D1407542

Books in the Life Long Ago Series

The Life Long Ago books are close-up views of ancient civilizations. Everyday life is brilliantly re-created in panoramic, authentic drawings and concise text. Each book is a rare visual experience. Each takes the reader into the reality and excitement of history and provides an extraordinary understanding of a people and their ways.

THE EGYPTIANS in the Middle Kingdom

Pictures by SHANE MILLER
Text by EDWARD OCHSENSCHLAGER

A fascinating trip through this ancient land where you will visit the lonely Pharaoh of Egypt, walk through the shop-lined streets of Memphis and journey past the great pyramids of Giza.

THE CAVE DWELLERS in the Old Stone Age

Pictures and Text by RICHARD M. POWERS

The pictures burst with life and strength. You feel the tense anticipation of the hunters as they gather before the magician in the ritual cave. You know the fear as they face a live mammoth, and realize they must kill or be killed.

THE ATHENIANS in the Classical Period

Pictures and Text by LEONARD WEISGARD

The beauty and reality of Athens is before you in the streets of the city as you visit an instrument maker's shop, join the crowds at the Panathenaic Stadium and stand before the Parthenon.

THE ROMANS in the Days of the Empire

Pictures and Text by SHANE MILLER

The mighty Roman Empire is vividly alive in the strength of these pictures. You take your seat among 45,000 spectators at the Colosseum. You follow a freedman home to his four-story apartment house and you feel the might of the Roman army as they prepare for battle.

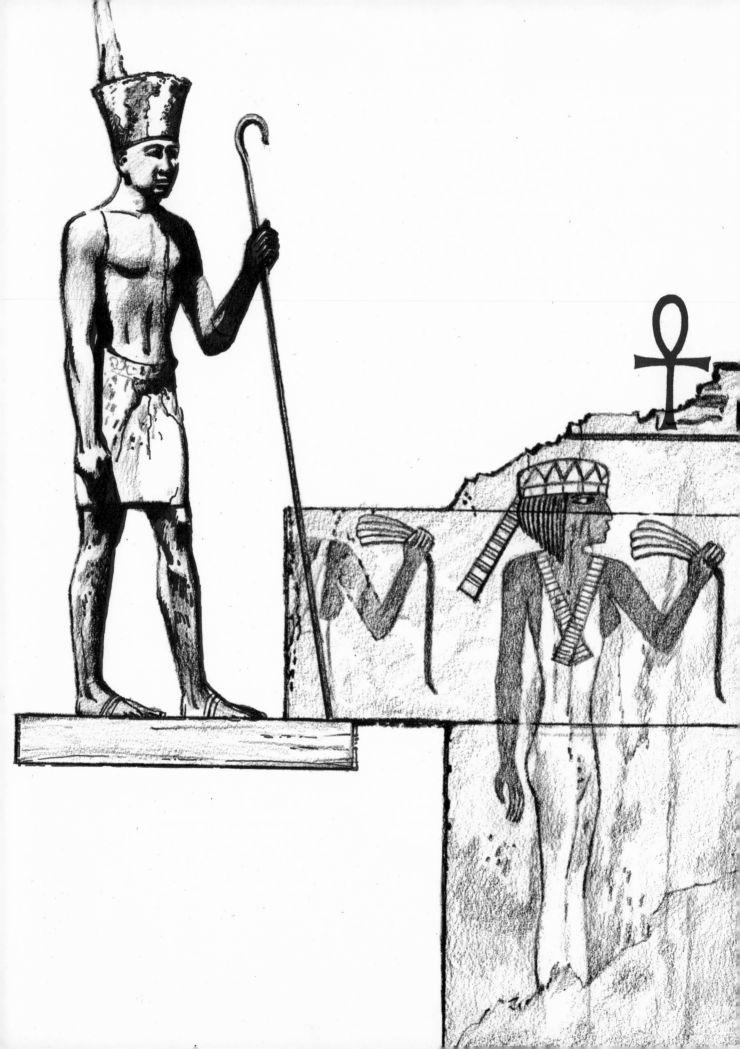

LIFE LONG AGO

Editorial and Historical Consultant **Edward Ochsenschlager**
ARCHAEOLOGIST AND LECTURER IN CLASSICS

THE EGYPTIANS
In the Middle Kingdom

Pictures SHANE MILLER

Text EDWARD OCHSENSCHLAGER

Education Consultant **Rosemary Daly**
LIBRARIAN, ETHICAL CULTURE SCHOOL, NEW YORK

COWARD-McCANN
New York

0110 UP

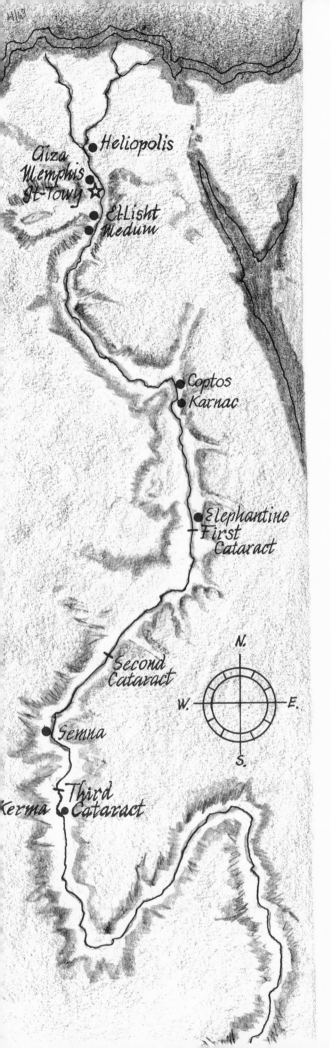

Praise to you, O Nile, who issues from the earth and comes to nourish Egypt. You give the fields to drink and make the people strong.

— HYMN TO THE NILE

Once a year the river Nile overflowed its banks, bringing water to the parched land. Then slowly the waters receded within the river's banks, leaving a layer of silt rich in minerals. This made the Nile valley the most fertile land of the ancient Mediterranean world. The Nile provided the Egyptian with all his necessities and many of his pleasures. It served as a road upon which he traveled for business, pleasure, and to pay homage to his gods. Rain, the Egyptians thought, came from a Nile set in the sky to lighten the misery of those less fortunate nations who did not have a Nile flowing through their land.

3

I stood upon the boundaries of the land and beheld its circuit.

— INSTRUCTION OF KING AMENEMHET

At Kerma, in the center of Nubian territory, and some miles south of the Egyptian frontier, the Egyptians established a fortified trading post known as "The Walls of Amenemhet, the Justified."

Kerma was perfectly situated for trade. To the south lay the fertile region of the Fourth Cataract. It could be reached in two days by donkey caravan. To the north the treacherous rapids of the Third Cataract prevented heavy shipping on the Nile. But there were good roads from Kerma which provided safe transport to the Second Cataract, where river traffic could safely be resumed.

Thousands of Nubians came to Kerma to trade with the Egyptians. They brought with them ivory, precious woods, slaves, fine stones, resins, oils, special grains, incense, and leopard skins.

So important was Kerma to the Pharaoh that he appointed a high-ranking official to govern it.

The king's official, retiring now that he is an old man, makes a last visit to the market before he begins his long journey down the Nile. Among his purchases is a young slave to serve him on his homeward voyage.

The products of the craftsmen at Kerma were much sought after in Egypt. An intermingling of Egyptian and African styles had resulted in textiles, pottery and jewelry of unusual design.

Rings of metal were sometimes used for exchange, but most trade was carried on by barter. People of rank were accompanied to the market by servants or slaves. The servants carried the heavy bronze rings on their arms, and goods for exchange in their hands. After purchases were made, they carried the parcels home for their masters.

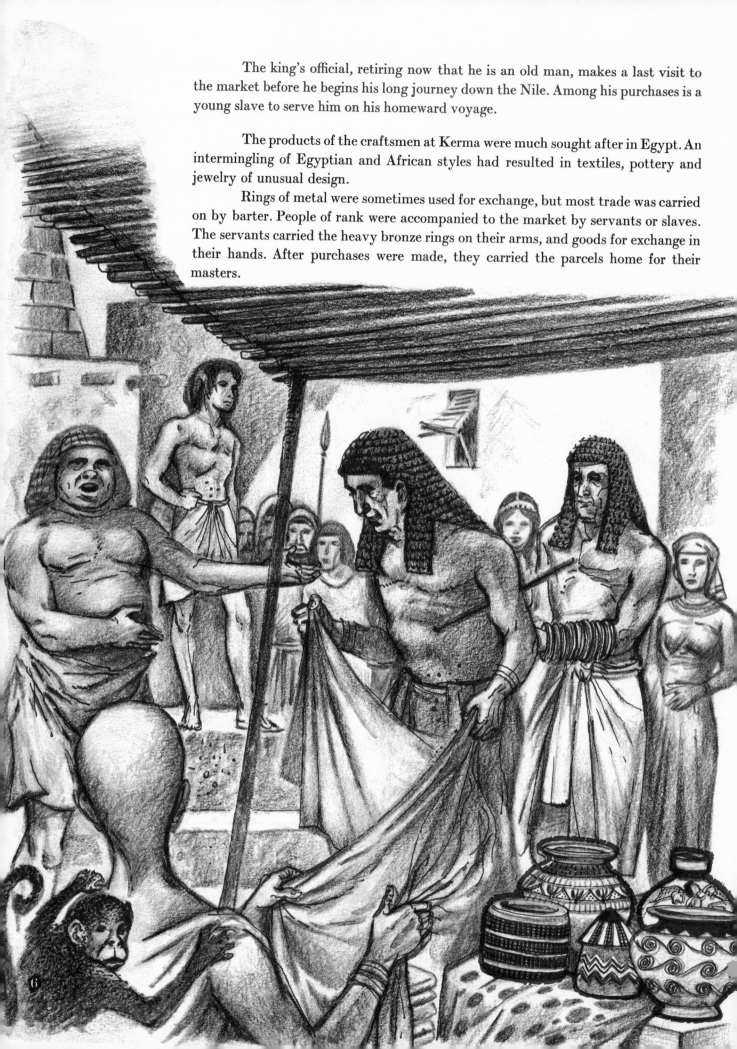

The officials of Kerma bid farewell to their respected governor.

There was a strong garrison of soldiers at Kerma. Trade with the Nubians was highly desired, but the Egyptian traders must be protected against possible attack by these fierce fighters.

The soldiers of the Egyptian army, whether slingers, spearmen, archers or axmen, were all light-armed infantry. Most of them were freeborn citizens serving the Pharaoh as professional soldiers, or levied and maintained by the provincial governors.

Egyptian soldiers were taught the principles of warfare in mock battles. Their commanders kept them in good physical condition by exercising them regularly in gymnastics and wrestling.

7

*Now, as for every son of mine who shall maintain this boundary, which my majesty
has made, he is my son.*

— Stele of Sesostris III at Semna

At Uronarti, just north of the Second Cataract, the governor and his retinue
change to a larger boat. The danger of the rapids is past.

Uronarti and nearby Semna were border fortresses at the southernmost
boundary of Egyptian occupation. Between here and Mirgissa, the people of Egypt
were protected against the Nubians by a series of strong fortifications. These fortified
cities were built and garrisoned by the soldiers. The Egyptian army was called upon
for public works and stone quarrying, as well as military duties.

An important official traveling on the Nile would have a kitchen boat, as well
as his personal traveling boat. At mealtime the kitchen boat would draw alongside to
serve him. Although these boats were rowed downstream, each was equipped with a
mast, spars and a square sail for going upstream with the wind.

PLAN
Fortress of
URONARTI

30 ft.
10 cm.

E S

W

9

Stand well with the Southern Land. Then the bearers of bags come to thee with gifts.
— Instruction for King Merikere

The governor's boats approach the "Nome," or district, of Elephantine, governed by a powerful hereditary prince.

The resources of the southern part of Egypt were indeed important to the Pharaohs.

Huge blocks of granite were quarried from the hills and dragged, with great effort, down a massive causeway to the Nile. The blocks were broken off from the cliffs by boring numerous holes along a prescribed line, driving wooden wedges into these, and then wetting the wedges. As the moist wedges expanded, the stone broke with a fairly smooth fracture. The stones were then roughly shaped to make them lighter and more easily transported.

Just south of Elephantine were copper mines. Bronze, made from tin and copper, was the basic metal medium of exchange throughout the ancient world.

At Karnak the governor goes ashore to pay his respects to the god Amon. The new slave accompanies him.

The Egyptians worshiped many gods, and each of these gods had many attributes. Amon was the protector of the poor and the helpless. He was also the god who separated justice from injustice. The father of Sesostris I had built a temple to Amon at Karnak, near Thebes. His son enlarged it. Soon Amon became the chief god of all Egypt.

The Egyptian thought that what was pleasing to his gods was good, what displeased them was evil. Although Egyptian ideas of right and wrong were sometimes different from modern ideas, most Egyptians were extremely concerned with morality.

Lord of Truth, father of the Gods, who made mankind, and created beasts.
— THE GREAT HYMN TO AMON

Early in August a great festival was held at Karnak. With much ceremony the image of the god Amon, in his golden bark, was brought forth from the holy of holies, or innermost sanctuary of the temple. In ancient Egypt, the image was not considered as the god himself. Indeed the name Amon meant "Hidden." Amon was an unseen god who might be anywhere or everywhere. His image was merely a convenient form in which he might make an appearance, if he chose.

Most of the year the image of the god was served within the sanctuary by his priests. It was awakened in the morning, bathed and anointed with oil. Incense was burned and offerings of food and drink were made before it.

He to whom men's hearts come nestling, who suffereth mankind to come out to him, who gladdens the Two Lands with his going forth.

— THE GREAT HYMN TO AMON

Surrounded by priests, and watched by the rejoicing populace, the god in his golden bark is carried to the banks of the Nile.

The god journeyed by boat across the Nile to the great funerary tomb of Neb-hepet-ra Mentuhotep, who had reunified Egypt one hundred years before. From above the tomb priests of Neb-hepet-ra kept watch for the god's approach, prepared to call out to the other priests and the people gathered below in expectation.

Overnight the image stayed within the funerary temple. Just as the god might make an appearance within his image if he chose, so the dead king could also appear in his statues or images within the temple. Thus, it was believed, they conversed with each other.

They tremble who behold the Nile in full flood. The fields laugh and the riverbanks are overflown. The god's offerings descend, the visage of man is bright, and the heart of the god rejoices.

— UTTERANCE 581, THE PYRAMID TEXTS

16

As the floodwaters of the Nile reach their full height, the governor continues his journey downstream.

At the height of the inundation, the waters of the Nile covered the valley. Only the houses, built on higher ground, and the trees stood out above the waters. On the hillocks, above the reach of the Nile, the livestock was gathered. If the waters did not rise high enough, the land yielded few crops and the people were hungry. If they rose too high, houses, possessions and livestock were swept downstream, which was as great a disaster.

It was important for men to know when the river would begin to rise, so they could make preparations. Through observation of the stars and of such natural occurrences as the flood, a calendar had been devised.

The Egyptian calendar was based on the most important phases of Egyptian agriculture. There were three seasons. The first was called the "Inundation," the second "Growth" and the third "Harvest." Because the Egyptian calendar year had only 365 days — a quarter of a day less than a true year — the times of the seasons eventually became displaced. Only once in every 1,460 years did the calendar and the astronomical year coincide. By simple observation of the moon and stars, however, the Egyptian was always able to predict the rise of the Nile with fair accuracy.

And he gave me a freight of myrrh . . . eye cosmetic, giraffes' tails, a large amount of incense, elephant tusks, greyhounds, monkeys, apes, and all goodly treasures.
— THE STORY OF THE SHIPWRECKED SAILOR

At Coptos the ship's crew goes ashore for provisions. The governor points out a returning caravan to the young slave.

Coptos was one of the busiest towns on the Nile. Here the caravan route to the east began and ended. The route stretched across the desert to the quarries of the Wady-el-Hammamat where hard stone (breccia and diorite) was obtained for the Pharaoh's buildings. From there it crossed the desert to Quesir, a port on the Red Sea, from which sea voyages were made to Punt, in what is now Ethiopia. The journey was difficult but very worthwhile. Many "goodly treasures" were to be found in Punt. The caravans brought back not only luxury goods to delight the court, but the very necessary incense burned in great quantities before the gods.

One of the members of the crew is ill and the governor has him carried to the house of a doctor. The man is not seriously ill: it is only an upset stomach. The doctor orders him to chew castor bean seeds and wash down the oil and seed pods with beer.

Egyptian doctors were in many ways accomplished men. They discovered many medicines and remedies which are still in use. Castor oil, for instance, is still used for upset stomachs. Another of their remedies, hartshorn, a form of ammonia extracted from deer antlers, was used to revive fainting women until a cheap way was found of making ammonia.

The doctor pulled teeth and filled cavities with a mixture of malachite, frankincense and yellow ochre. He set broken bones in splints, stitched gaping wounds and dressed them expertly. He knew and wrote about simple anatomy and could remove tumors and perform minor operations. Indeed, there is even evidence that delicate, complicated operations were successfully performed on the skull.

Not all Egyptian medical practices were so scientific. They thought many diseases were caused by evil spirits and sometimes used unpleasant remedies to drive these spirits out of the body. One remedy consisted of animal fat and dung swallowed with beer. Such remedies were accompanied by magic charms and incantations, and were probably sometimes effective. They encouraged the superstitious patient to think that he was getting better.

Every cook was at his task, and I set out and sailed; and the men kneaded and brewed beside me . . .

— THE STORY OF SINUHE

20

The young slave is selected by the governor to be his personal servant.

Slavery was practiced in Egypt. Yet, during the Middle Kingdom, there was an ideal of the dignity of man which could reach down even into the ranks of the slaves. Some slaves fared better than others, but even under a bad master ability and intelligence were often rewarded with more interesting and responsible jobs.

As the Nile receded within its banks, each bit of ground as it appeared above the water was prepared with a plow or hoe for the sowing of the grain. The plow consisted of a pointed wooden plowshare, a double handle and a pole, to which the animals that drew it were attached. The plow was usually drawn by two oxen or two cows. Sometimes the animals pulled the plow with their shoulders. At other times the crossbar at the end of the plow pole was lashed to the base of their horns. Small calves often followed the cows to the field but were muzzled to prevent their seeking nourishment.

Where the soil was light and loose the hoe took the place of the plow. The hoe, like the plow, was made of wood. It consisted of a rounded or pointed pick attached to a handle with a twisted thong. The hoe was shaped like the letter A, and required the user to bend over his work.

When the ground was prepared, the sower scattered seed from a large basket he carried in his left hand. The seed was either allowed to sprout where it fell, or sheep, goats or pigs were driven over it, treading the seed into the soil.

At Lisht the tomb of the Pharaoh Sesostris I is under construction. The governor, like all Egyptians, is eager to see it.

The tomb, in which the soul might find food and lodging on earth, was very important to the ancient Egyptians. It was constructed with lavish care. The Pharaoh's tomb was especially important, as his rebirth in the realms of the gods was vital to the well-being of the nation.

To build the tomb and mortuary temple of the Pharaoh was no easy undertaking. Huge stones must be quarried and brought from afar. Then they must be carefully shaped and fitted into place.

As much effort was expended upon the decoration of the interior as upon the structure itself. Scenes from everyday life and records of the great deeds of the occupant were carved or painted — sometimes both — along with ritual prayers. In complete charge was the architect, upon whose inventiveness and mastery of his craft the end result depended.

22

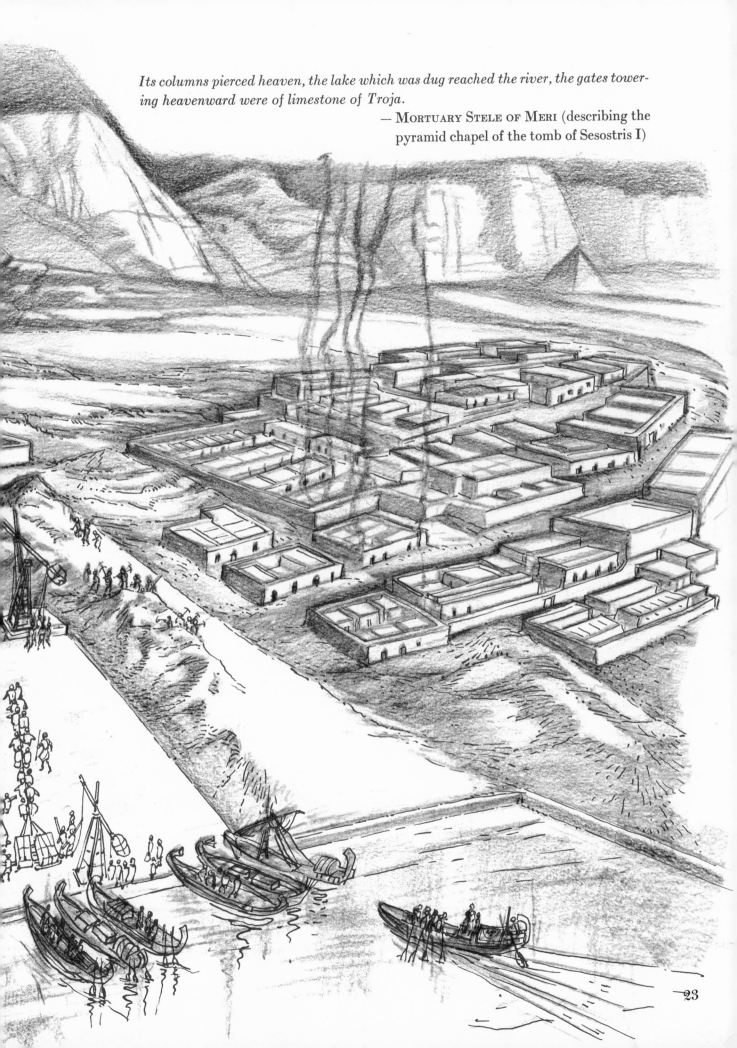

Its columns pierced heaven, the lake which was dug reached the river, the gates towering heavenward were of limestone of Troja.

— MORTUARY STELE OF MERI (describing the pyramid chapel of the tomb of Sesostris I)

At Lisht a town was laid out to house the workmen, skilled laborers, the priests and royal overseers. The workmen lived in mud brick houses, as did all Egyptians. Only the temples and tombs were made of more durable stone. The rich mud of the Nile furnished the material for the bricks. Once a brick was formed, it was dried in the sun. A mud brick house covered with protective plaster would last for many years.

Able-bodied men were conscripted in critical times for war, as well as in normal times for public works such as the Pharaoh's tomb. These conscripted men have often been thought of as slaves, and perhaps they were in earlier times. But now, in the Middle Kingdom, they were not. Slaves were still used for purely physical work, but for skilled work an army of craftsmen and artisans was necessary. Artisans were divided into shifts, each under a foreman, and ancient records show that absenteeism was frequent, often on very flimsy excuses.

At last the governor reaches the royal palace, where he is to make his final report to the king.

The palace of Sesostris I, the king of Upper and Lower Egypt, was at It-Towy. It was large and splendid, and so solidly built that the father of Sesostris I claimed that eternity was afraid because it could not be destroyed.

Upper and Lower Egypt were very different, and each was ruled by an entirely separate set of officials. However, they were united in the person of the god-king, who held supreme power in both. The king owned, controlled and defended all Egypt. It was his duty to nourish his people and seek out useful and beneficial things he might do for them.

I built a house adorned with gold; its ceilings are of lapis lazuli...the doors are copper and the bolts of bronze; they are for endless time, and eternity is afraid of them.
— INSTRUCTION OF KING AMENEMHET

Within the palace the king and the queen are awakened with a hymn, as is the image of the royal serpent, which is a part of the king's crown.

Morning was a busy time for the queen. Like all women of this time she spent many hours dressing and applying make-up. Ladies in the Middle Kingdom wore elaborate wigs, plaited into tresses and threaded with gold tubes. They used green eye shadow made from malachite. Their eyes were underlined, and their eyebrows painted with a dark paste called kohl, or antimony. Henna was used to dye the fingernails a reddish-orange color. They painted their lips, and used many lotions on their skin.

Egyptian women wore a variety of jewelry; armlets, bracelets, earrings, necklaces and rings on their fingers and toes. The queen's jewelry was gold, and either decorated with cloisonnée work, or inlaid with lapis lazuli, carnelian, turquoise, garnets and precious stones.

Women were not only the wives of men, but also their friends and companions. They appeared with their husbands in private company and public ceremonies. By law they possessed equal rights with men. A woman could even ascend the throne and become the sole ruler of Egypt.

The governor, while he visits the Pharaoh, leaves the boy in the Royal School for Scribes.

The Egyptians wrote with pictures which are called hieroglyphs. Originally each picture stood for a word or concept. Soon some pictures came to stand for letters, and the Egyptians developed an alphabet. Although we can read Egyptian writing, we cannot always pronounce their words because they had no signs for vowels.

The life of a student in the school for scribes was not easy. It usually took between ten and twelve years to learn thoroughly the hieroglyphic characters and how to form correct sentences with them. Over and over again the student copied such maxims as the one above, until he could write them perfectly. This repetition taught him not only the construction of words and sentences, but also the homely truths that had been handed down by great men to guide the lives of their descendants. If a boy was lazy or careless he was beaten.

But it was worth the hard work. Reading and writing were high accomplishments in Egypt, and few people mastered this difficult task. Only a scribe was eligible for high offices in the government or army.

The scribe sat cross-legged; his short skirt stretched tightly across his knees formed a kind of desk. Beside him was his palette, fitted with a slot for his brushes. He made his brush from a section of rush stem by chewing the end until the fibers were broken and could be shaped into a point. Attached to the palette were small squares of ink made from finely ground red ochre, or soot, mixed with gum and water, and dried into bricks.

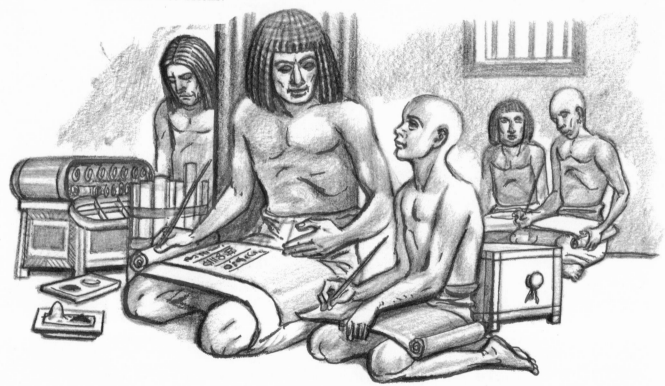

Be not arrogant because of your knowledge, and have no confidence that you are a learned man. Take counsel with the ignorant as well as with the wise, for the limits of art cannot be reached, and no artist fully possesses his skill.

— INSTRUCTION OF PTAHHOTEP

The governor, surrounded by the court, kisses the ground before the king.

He was a lonely king, this Pharaoh of Egypt, for he was considered a god. A few royal servants, probably of his own family, were the only persons allowed to approach the king closely. An ordinary human being, if touched by the awful majesty of the god, his clothing or his shadow, might suffer great harm.

A mere mortal never spoke directly to the king, and many ways were devised to avoid direct reference to him. For instance, the word "Pharaoh" comes from "Per-aa," which means "The Great House." Thus one referred to the house of the king, rather than to the actual man.

He is the one who makes the two lands brighter than does the sun. He is the one who makes the land greener than does a high Nile. He has filled the two lands with strength and life.

— INSTRUCTION OF KING AMENEMHET

Memphis, the administrative capital of Upper and Lower Egypt, was also a center of trade. Wine, olive oil, silver, copper, tin, obsidian and lapis lazuli were brought here from the Mediterranean, as well as merchandise from the Red Sea, Nubia and Egypt itself.

One of the most important imports was cedarwood from Lebanon. Nowhere in Egypt was to be found the good quality of lumber needed for the construction of the palace and temples, the wooden coffins and the large boats which kept peace on the Nile.

No one was hungry in my years; no one was thirsty in them.
— INSTRUCTION OF KING AMENEMHET

The governor stops at the city of Memphis, which is not far from the palace of It-Towy. The markets here are famous throughout Egypt.

I made the four winds that every man might breathe thereof.
— Coffin Texts

The market streets at Memphis are lined with the shops of craftsmen.

Many craftsmen plied their trade in ancient Egypt. During the Middle Kingdom they produced jewelry of exquisite skill, beautifully decorated pottery, and furniture of wood inlaid with ivory.

It is good to think that the idea of the equality of men, found in ancient Egypt only in the Middle Kingdom, was responsible for the flowering of the craftsman's art.

34

On the last part of the long homeward journey, the governor's boats pass the great pyramids of Giza.

The great pyramids, built in the Fourth Dynasty, centuries before this time, were objects of awe and veneration to Middle Kingdom Egyptians. The largest had been built by the Pharaoh Khufu. The Great Pyramid covered 12½ acres and was 481 feet tall. Over 2,300,000 blocks of stone, some weighing over 2½ tons, were used to build this 6,250,000-ton monument. The builders lacked wheeled vehicles, pulleys or cranes. They maneuvered each block into place with sloping ramps of brick and earth, levers, cradles, sledges and ropes. Yet they had managed to dress and fit the outer blocks so skillfully that the joint between blocks was only one-fiftieth of an inch wide.

Physically Egypt had changed little since these pyramids were erected. Sculptors and builders imitated the old forms. War, along with the enjoyment of peace, was still much as it had been. Men still hunted, fished and earned their daily livelihood in much the same ways. But in the Middle Kingdom there was a new emphasis on social justice and righteous dealings with one's fellow men.

I made the great flood waters, that the poor man might have rights in them like the great man . . .

— COFFIN TEXTS

Be not evil; it is good to be kindly. Cause your monument to endure through the love of thee.

— INSTRUCTION FOR KING MERIKERE

The governor arrives at his country estate and steps ashore amid a multitude of familiar sights. His family, overseers, farmers, musicians and slaves greet him with undisguised joy. The governor's land stretches far into the distance. The fertility of his fields and the health of his livestock are dependent on the waters of the Nile which have brought him home.

Life on a country estate in Middle Kingdom Egypt was pleasant for everyone if the master was a man of his times. Masters had always been dispensers of justice. But justice at this period was not primarily concerned with the carrying out of laws. A far greater emphasis was placed on seeking out what was best for each man according to his individual needs. A master who dispensed this kind of justice was long remembered by his workmen with love and gratitude.

The governor is happy to be in his own house once more and to assume personal management of his estate. To the boy everything is new and exciting.

The estate of a wealthy Egyptian was entirely self-sufficient. Within the rambling dwelling were the rooms which housed the master, his family, and the household servants. There were also lush patios, or walled gardens, which served as outdoor living rooms.

Close to the house, or perhaps actually attached to it, were the buildings which serviced the household. There was a bakery, where grain was ground into flour and made into bread. Close by was the brewery, where other grain was mixed with water and allowed to ferment into a kind of beer. The butchery provided the meat of cattle and fowl for the kitchen, where it was prepared for serving. There was also a building where weavers made fine linens for all the household needs.

On large estates it was sometimes difficult for the owner to keep a record of the numbers of his livestock. They were often cared for by numerous herdsmen, each of whom had the responsibility of only a few animals. Taking count of his herds, therefore, was a complicated task for the master, and generally performed on a day set aside for this purpose. Each herdsman, in turn, drove his cattle before the owner and his scribes. The scribes entered each new calf in the register and the owner checked to make certain that each animal was being cared for properly.

Most of the year the cattle were pastured in open fields. During the annual flood they were brought into the farmyards and kept in sheds and pens, or driven to higher land which stood out above the water. Here they were fed on grasses cut and dried for this purpose. Before butchering they were again confined and force-fed by attendants who stood alongside them, stuffing food into the mouths of the cattle.

Flax was widely grown in Egypt. Men harvested the stalks and immersed them in pools of water warmed by the sun, using stones to weigh them down. When the rind of the stalk became loose they removed the stalks from the water, thoroughly dried them in the sun, and afterwards beat them on stone slabs with wooden mallets. The rind and outer fibers were combed away to use for lamp wicks. The inner part, of a fine white quality, was combed for weaving.

Both men and women were employed in spinning the fibers into thread, and weaving the thread into fabric. Thread was made on a wooden spindle, and woven into cloth on a loom. In weaving, the threads were interlaced at right angles by means of a shuttle which was used to pass the woof (transverse threads) between the warp (longitudinal threads). The woof threads were then pressed firmly into the warp.

Egyptians wove cotton and wool, as well as linen. Linen, however, was worn by all classes and priests were allowed to wear nothing else while officiating. It was also used as wrappings for mummies.

Linen cloth was naturally white but it could be dyed solidly or in stripes or patterns. Sometimes designs were woven into the fabric with colored threads.

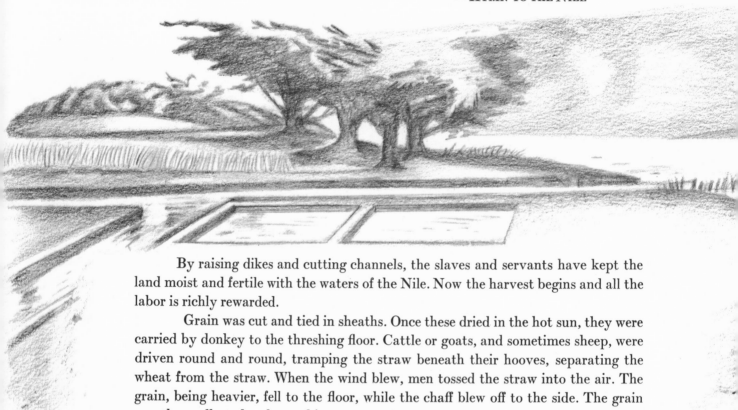

By raising dikes and cutting channels, the slaves and servants have kept the land moist and fertile with the waters of the Nile. Now the harvest begins and all the labor is richly rewarded.

Grain was cut and tied in sheaths. Once these dried in the hot sun, they were carried by donkey to the threshing floor. Cattle or goats, and sometimes sheep, were driven round and round, tramping the straw beneath their hooves, separating the wheat from the straw. When the wind blew, men tossed the straw into the air. The grain, being heavier, fell to the floor, while the chaff blew off to the side. The grain was then collected and stored in a granary.

In the swamplands papyrus was cut by men in small boats. On the dry land other men cut the pith of the papyrus into thin strips and laid them on a flat surface in two layers. In the first layer the fibers were laid vertically and in the second layer horizontally. The two layers were bound together with glue, water and pressure, and the surface was polished smooth. The papyrus sheets made in this way were used for writing paper, either singly or pasted end to end and rolled into scrolls.

Although the governor has not been feeling well for some time, he is giving a banquet. For the young slave it is a very special banquet. Tonight he will be given his freedom. The governor has invited many friends to serve as witnesses.

It was not unusual for a master to free especially intelligent and able slaves. A slave was freed by a simple declaration before witnesses.

Guests arriving for a banquet were greeted by their host. They washed their hands with water from a large stone jar. Servants presented them garlands of flowers and cups of wine. Dishes of food were placed on low tables around the room and passed by servant girls. There were dates, grapes, figs, cakes of different kinds and roasted fowls. Guests ate with their fingers and a servant passed among them with a bowl of water and a linen towel for washing and drying their hands. An orchestra played flutes, harps, lutes and lyres while dancing girls entertained the guests.

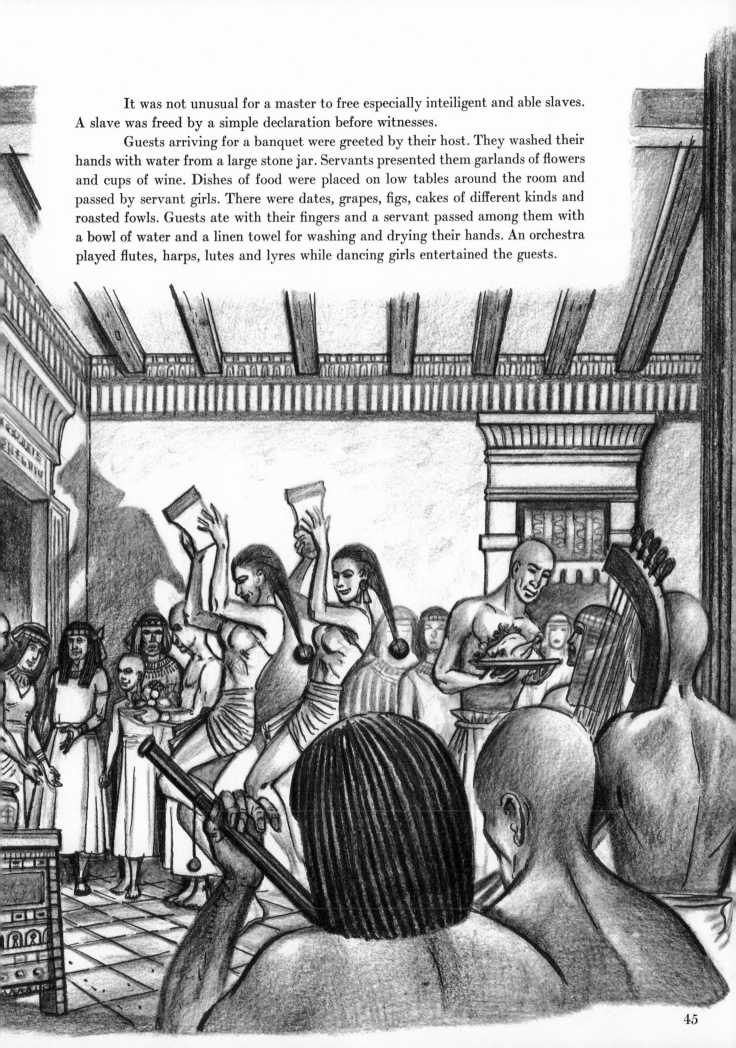

Death is before me today as a well-trodden path, as when a man returns from the war unto his own house.

— DISPUTE WITH HIS SOUL OF ONE WHO IS TIRED OF LIFE

The governor does not get better. He and those he loves best know that his life on earth is nearly over.

The Egyptian thought of death not as the end of life, but rather as the beginning of a new life. He thoroughly enjoyed life on earth, and did not look forward to death as an escape from it, but he believed that when death came, a happy and successful life on earth could be continued in a new way in the next world.

The Egyptian thought of himself as having two indestructible "souls." When he died, his *ba*, or ghost, left his body in the form of a bird. The ba was that part of a man's personality which, after death, could effectively maintain contact between his body in the tomb, the surviving family and his *ka* in another world. The ka, man's divine nature and vital force, was born as his twin, stayed with him during life, and preceded him in death to arrange for his successful existence with the gods in the other world.

A man did not automatically attain eternal blessedness. He must, after death, appear before a tribunal of gods, where his good was weighed against his bad. Only if the good outweighed the bad could a man hope to enjoy the eternal blessings of death.

The funerary boats set sail for the governor's tomb: his eternal home. The lector, or reader priest, stands before the mummy reciting sacred texts from his scroll.

It was essential that the ba have a well preserved body if it was to have an existence in the tomb. If the ba was preserved intact, a man could eternally experience the pleasures of his life on earth. For men of rank the mummification process took seventy to eighty days. All the organs were removed and placed in jars, with the exception of the heart, which was believed to be the center of all life and intelligence. The brain was removed through the nose with a long hook. The body was then soaked in natron (soda), its cavity filled with wads of linen, sawdust and resin, and the whole treated with aromatic resins.

After this process the mummy was carefully wrapped in layers of linen bandages, sheets and padding, and adorned with funerary jewelry. It was placed full length in a coffin of wood shaped like the human body. Amid the wailing of mourning women, who were often professionals hired for this purpose, the mummy was carried from the home to the tomb. The procession included the mourning family, friends, servants and the priests, along with the funerary furniture and offerings for the ba.

This is what my ba said to me . . . When you reach the West and your body is united with the earth, then I will alight . . . Let us have an abode together.
— DISPUTE WITH HIS SOUL OF ONE WHO IS TIRED OF LIFE

The governor's tomb was symbolically built to the west of the Nile. Because the sun set in the west, the Egyptians thought the "next world" was to be sought in this direction. When the funeral procession arrived at the tomb, sacrifices were offered, more sacred texts recited by the lector, and ceremonial dances performed. A meal was prepared to give nourishment to the reanimated ba. A ceremonial entrance into the tomb was then made, and the coffin was placed on its left side in an outer coffin.

The funerary objects were arranged within the tomb. There were small models of servants, some carrying food, and models of the breweries, butcheries, bakeries and kitchens where food was prepared. Models of soldiers were added for protection of the deceased, ship models for his transportation, model tools, and other model scenes from his estate. By magic rites these miniature models were made capable of serving the ba as the originals had served the man on earth. Games he had enjoyed in life, ceremonial staves and scepters, real furniture and plates filled with food offerings were also placed near the coffin. When all were in place, the tomb was sealed.

In the tomb the ba had needs similar to those it had in this world. The mortuary liturgy required the presence of a priest whose livelihood was provided for from portions of the dead man's estate. The ritual followed a daily pattern. There was a ceremonial "opening of the mouth" of the deceased's image which was a part of the funerary temple. This rite was concerned with the nourishment of the ba. The image was also anointed and censed. Only when these ceremonies were properly performed could the ba maintain contact with the ka in heaven.

A man was considered lucky if posterity saw to it that these rituals were properly performed, and doubly lucky if his descendants passed on from generation to generation the wisdom he had passed on to them.

It is this which teaches a man to speak to posterity that it may hear it, and to be an artist, one who has heard what is good, and who now on his part speaks to posterity that it may hear it.

— INSTRUCTION OF PTAHHOTEP

EGYPTIAN GODS

RA (RE) (rah, rā)
— the sun-god, lord of the sky, creator and ruler of the world. He is generally represented with a sun disk on his head. Egyptians believed that he was the father of every Pharaoh.

AMON (ah'mŭn)
— began to be an important god in the Twelfth Dynasty. He soon became the foremost god of Egypt and king of the gods. Eventually associated with Ra, he took the name Amon-Ra and in the minds of Egyptians superseded Ra as the creator and ruler of the universe. Amon is represented as a man, as a man with a ram's head, or as a ram.

OSIRIS (ō·sīr'ĭs)
— the god of the dead. In the story of his death and resurrection, Egyptians found the basis of their belief in a life after death. He is usually represented as a man swathed in white mummy wrappings.

ISIS (ī'sĭs)
— the wife of Òsiris and protector of the dead, possessed of magical powers. She brought about the resurrection of Osiris through the rites of embalmment which she performed for the first time.

HORUS (hō'rŭs)
— the son of Osiris whom Isis conceived by magic after her husband's death. After a long war with Set, his father's slayer, a tribunal of the gods awarded him victory and declared him ruler of Upper and Lower Egypt. He was regarded as the ancestor of the Pharaohs.

HATHOR (hăth'or)
— the wife of Horus, the protectress of women, and goddess of music, dance, joy, and love. She is represented as a human with cow's-horns headdress, as a human with a cow's head, or as a cow.

ANUBIS (ă·nū'bĭs)
— the conductor of souls to the land of the dead. He invented funerary rites and mummy wrappings to preserve the body of Osiris. Anubis is represented as a bushy-tailed black jackal or as a man with the head of a jackal or dog.

SET
— the brother and adversary of Osiris. In late times, the god of evil and destruction. He is shown as a man with the face or head of a strange beast characterized by a long, thin, curved snout and square-cut ears. His skin is white and his hair red — a most unseemly combination to an ancient Egyptian.

PTAH (p'tah)
— the patron of artisans and artists, and the smelter of metal. Near his temple a live bull called Apis was tended by priests. The bull was thought to be an incarnation of Ptah.

SEKHET (sĕk'ĕt)
— the wife of Ptah and the bloodthirsty goddess of war and battle. She is usually represented as a woman with the head of a lioness or as a lioness.

THOTH (thōth) — the moon god and patron of wisdom, science, literature, and the arts. He was also the god of all inventions, the messenger of the gods and the keeper of all divine records. Usually he is represented as a man with the head of an ibis, as an ibis, or as a dog-headed ape.

MONT (MENTHU) (měn′thōo) — the sun-god of war who attained tremendous popularity in Upper Egypt during the Eleventh Dynasty. He is represented as a man with the head of a falcon or a bull.

HAPI (hah′pē) — the god of the Nile, represented as a fat but vigorous man with large flabby breasts.

BES (běs) — the god of marriage.

BUTO (bū′tō) — the protective goddess of Lower Egypt.

MAAT (mă·aht′) — the goddess of truth or justice.

MESKHENT (měs′kěnt) — the goddess of childbirth.

NEKHEBET (někʹě·bět) — the protective goddess of Upper Egypt.

RENENET (rěn·ěn′ět) — the goddess of nourishment who presided over the suckling of babies.

SIGNIFICANT DATES IN THE MIDDLE KINGDOM

2258 B.C.	The government of the Old Kingdom in Egypt collapsed and the country was plunged into chaos.
2134 B.C.	Intef I declared himself king in Thebes, the capital of Upper Egypt, and founded the Eleventh Dynasty.
2133 B.C.	Neferkara founded the Tenth Dynasty in Lower Egypt to the north. War broke out between the two dynasties.
ca. 2052 B.C.	Mentuhotep II conquered the northern Pharaohs, and united all Egypt under his rule.
1991 B.C.	Amenemhet overthrew the last Pharaoh of the Eleventh Dynasty, seized the throne and founded the Twelfth Dynasty.
1991–1981 B.C.	The capital was moved from Thebes to Lisht, about 25 miles south of Memphis.
1962–1928 B.C.	A series of military expeditions under Sesostris I extended Egyptian control beyond the Second Cataract. Garrisoned fortifications were built to protect the southern trade routes. To the north a vigorous trade was carried on with Mediterranean peoples.
1928–1895 B.C.	Amenemhet II made many economic and agricultural improvements in Egypt. He abandoned his predecessors' programs of military expansion and consolidation in the conquered territories.
1895–1879 B.C.	Sesostris II continued the work of Amenemhet II and began a great project of land reclamation in the Faiyum basin.
1879–1841 B.C.	Sesostris III waged successful wars in Palestine and Nubia, and Nubia became a province of Egypt. At home he established the absolute power of the Pharaoh in every part of his realm.
1841–1792 B.C.	Amenemhet III completed the project of land reclamation in the Faiyum. Since that time, this area has been the most fertile in all Egypt.
1778 B.C.	Egypt collapsed into chaos under weak kings. In 1675 B.C., the throne was seized by an Asiatic king, and Egypt was ruled by the Hyksos for more than one hundred years.

CHRONOLOGICAL TABLE

PREHISTORIC PERIOD	Before 4000 B.C.
PREDYNASTIC PERIOD	4000–3200 B.C.

EARLY DYNASTIC PERIOD

Dynasty I	3200–2980 B.C.
Dynasty II	2980–2780 B.C.
Dynasty III	2780–2680 B.C.

OLD KINGDOM

Dynasty IV	2680–2565 B.C.
Dynasty V	2565–2420 B.C.
Dynasty VI	2420–2258 B.C.

FIRST INTERMEDIATE PERIOD

Dynasty VII	2258 B.C.
Dynasty VIII	2258–2232 B.C.
Dynasty IX	2232–2133 B.C.
Dynasty X	2133–2052 B.C.

MIDDLE KINGDOM

Dynasty XI

Intef I	2134–2131 B.C.
Intef II	2131–2082 B.C.
Intef III	2082–2079 B.C.
Mentuhotep I	2079–2061 B.C.
Mentuhotep II	2061–2010 B.C.
Mentuhotep III	2010–1998 B.C.
Mentuhotep IV	1993–1991 B.C.

Dynasty XII

Amenemhet I	1991–1962 B.C.
Sesostris I	1972–1928 B.C.
(co-regent with Amenemhet I for ten years)	
Amenemhet II	1930–1895 B.C.
(co-regent with Sesostris I for two years)	
Sesostris II	1898–1879 B.C.
(co-regent with Amenemhet II for three years)	
Sesostris III	1879–1841 B.C.
Amenemhet III	1841–1792 B.C.
Amenemhet IV	1792–1782 B.C.
Queen Sebek-nefru	1782–1778 B.C.

SECOND INTERMEDIATE PERIOD

Dynasty XIII	1778–1625 B.C.
Dynasty XIV	1778–1595 B.C.
Dynasty XV	1675–1570 B.C.
Dynasty XVI	1660–1600 B.C.
Dynasty XVII	1600–1570 B.C.

NEW KINGDOM

Dynasty XVIII	1570–1320 B.C.
Dynasty XIX	1320–1200 B.C.
Dynasty XX	1200–1085 B.C.

LATE PERIOD

Dynasty XXI	1085–950 B.C.
Dynasty XXII	950–730 B.C.
Dynasty XXIII	817–730 B.C.
Dynasty XXIV	730–715 B.C.
Dynasty XXV	730–663 B.C.
Dynasty XXVI	663–525 B.C.
Dynasty XXVII	525–404 B.C.
First Persian Domination	
Dynasty XXVIII	404–398 B.C.
Dynasty XXIX	398–378 B.C.
Dynasty XXX	378–341 B.C.
Dynasty XXXI	341–332 B.C.
Second Persian Domination	

PTOLEMAIC PERIOD — 332–30 B.C.

Conquest of Egypt by Alexander the Great — 332 B.C.

ROMAN PERIOD — 30 B.C.–364 A.D.

FOR FURTHER READING

Coolidge, Olivia, *Egyptian Adventures;* illus. by Joseph Low. Houghton, 1954
Stories about people of the New Kingdom, 1600 B.C.–1100 B.C.

Cottrell, Leonard, *Land of the Pharaohs*; illus. by Richard Powers. World, 1960

Falls, C. B., author-artist, *The First 3000 Years*. Viking, 1960
A truly beautiful book covering the ancient civilizations of the Tigris-Euphrates and Nile River valleys and the Mediterranean Sea

Fawcett, Raymond, ed., *How Did They Live? Egypt;* photographs by Robert Benchley. Boston, 1953
How people thought and behaved in Egypt 1,200 years before Christ

Glubok, Shirley, *The Art of Ancient Egypt;* illus. with reproductions. Atheneum, 1962
An art book that has useful background material for a study of Egypt

Jones, Ruth Fosdick, *Boy of the Pyramids;* illus. by Dorothy Bayley Morse. Random, 1952
The Egypt of Khufu revealed through this story of two children of Memphis who saw the Pyramids being built

McGraw, Eloise Jarvis, *Mara, Daughter of the Nile*. Coward-McCann, 1953
An intriguing novel set in the time of Queen Hatshepsut

Mayer, Josephine, and Prideux, Tom, *Never to Die: The Egyptians in Their Own Words*. Viking, 1938
The life of the people of Egypt revealed through their own ancient literature

Meadowcroft, Enid (La Monte), *The Gift of the River: A History of Ancient Egypt;* illus. by Katherine Dewey. Crowell, 1937
A young people's account of Egypt from earliest recorded history to the downfall of old Egypt

Robinson, Charles Alexander, *The First Book of Ancient Egypt;* illus. by Lili Rethi. Watts, 1961

Shealer, John M., *The Sycamore Warrior*. Dutton, 1960
A mystery story set in Ancient Egypt

Sellman, R. R., *Ancient Egypt*. Roy, 1960
A brief history beginning in prehistoric times and ending with the Arab conquest in 640 A.D.

INDEX

This is a partially annotated Index. Where no annotation occurs, the text is fully explanatory. Italic numerals designate page reference to pictures.